SPOTLIGHT ON OUR FUTURE

FOOD CHALLENGES AND OUR FUTURE

SABRINA ADAMS

NEW YORK

Published in 2022 by The Rosen Publishing Group, Inc.
29 East 21st Street, New York, NY 10010

Copyright © 2022 by The Rosen Publishing Group, Inc.

First Edition

All rights reserved. No part of this book may be reproduced in any form without permission in writing from the publisher, except by a reviewer.

Editor: Theresa Emminizer
Book Design: Michael Flynn

Photo Credits: Cover Thatree Thitivongvaroon/Moment/Getty Images; (series background) jessicahyde/Shutterstock.com; p. 04 Monkey Business Images/Shutterstock.com; p. 5 nito/Shutterstock.com; p. 7 (Upton Sinclair) Buyenlarge/Archive Photos/Getty Images; p. 7 (book) Bettmann/Getty Images; p. 8 iliuta goean/Shutterstock.com; p. 9 selimaksan/iStock/Getty Images; p. 10 WIN-Initiative/Stone/Getty Images; p. 11 The Washington Post/Getty Images; p. 12 Gestalt Imagery/Shutterstock.com; p. 13 symbiot/Shutterstock.com; p. 14 PixieMe/Shutterstock.com; p. 15 (alfalfa sprouts) Ildi Papp/Shutterstock.com; p. 15 (lentils) monticello/Shutterstock.com; p. 16 El Nariz/Shutterstock.com; p. 17 courtesy of choosemyplate.gov; p. 18 Antonina Vlasova/Shutterstock.com; p. 19 Rawpixel.com/Shutterstock.com; p. 21 Rawpixel/iStock/Getty Images; p. 22 fstop123/iStock/Getty Images; p. 23 mythja/Shutterstock.com; p. 25 Niall Carson/PA Images/Getty Images; p. 27 Sundry Photography/Shutterstock.com; p. 28 Africa Studio/Shutterstock.com; p. 29 https://commons.wikimedia.org/wiki/File:Obama_signs_FSMA_into_Law.jpg; p. 30 kryzhov/Shutterstock.com.

Cataloging-in-Publication Data

Names: Adams, Sabrina.
Title: Food challenges and our future / Sabrina Adams.
Description: New York : PowerKids Press, 2022. | Series: Spotlight on our future | Includes glossary and index.
Identifiers: ISBN 9781725323995 (pbk.) | ISBN 9781725324022 (library bound) | ISBN 9781725324008 (6pack)
Subjects: LCSH: Food security--Juvenile literature. | Food--Juvenile literature. | Food industry and trade--Juvenile literature.
Classification: LCC HD9000.5 A33 2022 | DDC 363.8--dc23

Manufactured in the United States of America

Some of the images in this book illustrate individuals who are models. The depictions do not imply actual situations or events.

CPSIA Compliance Information: Batch #CSPK22. For further information contact Rosen Publishing, New York, New York at 1-800-237-9932.

CONTENTS

A WORLD OF FOOD 4

THE BUSINESS OF FOOD 6

FOOD AROUND THE WORLD 8

FIXING FOOD DESERTS 10

WATCHING OUR WATER FOOTPRINT 12

FOOD AND FAIR TRADE 14

THE AVERAGE AMERICAN DIET 16

FOODS AROUND THE WORLD 18

TO THE GROCERY STORE 20

DIET AND LIFESTYLE 22

THE FIGHT FOR FOOD 24

NEW FARMING METHODS 26

HOW CAN I HELP? 28

THE FUTURE OF FOOD 30

GLOSSARY 31

INDEX 32

PRIMARY SOURCE LIST 32

WEBSITES 32

CHAPTER ONE

A WORLD OF FOOD

All people need food to live. In fact, the average adult needs between 2,000 and 2,500 calories a day. However, in some places, not everyone has enough to eat. When a person doesn't know where their next meal is coming from, that's called food insecurity. Today, there are more than 821 million people in the world who are regularly underfed.

The world population is growing every day. Unless we act now, in time, there may not be enough food for everyone.

There's more than enough food produced to feed everyone on the planet. In fact, there's more than 1½ times enough. However, not everyone can get the food they need. This is called food scarcity. In addition, a lot of the world's food is wasted. About a third of the food produced every year is thrown away. That's about 1.3 billion tons (1.2 billion mt) of food.

CHAPTER TWO

THE BUSINESS OF FOOD

Making sure everyone has enough to eat has always been a focus of society. Civilizations created farming practices to grow and harvest crops. During the 1800s, new inventions allowed food to be shipped around the world without going bad.

During this time, food also began to be processed and packaged in factories. Conditions in food-packing plants weren't always clean or safe. In 1906, a novel called *The Jungle* described real-life problems in the meatpacking industry. It showed the harsh and dirty conditions within factories. Readers were angry and upset and began to call for change. That same year, President Theodore Roosevelt signed a bill into law that made the food industry safer.

Today, there are both state and federal laws meant to make sure food is safe. That includes the way people handle food.

After Upton Sinclair's *The Jungle* was released, people asked the White House to help make changes in the food industry.

CHAPTER THREE

FOOD AROUND THE WORLD

Right now, the way plants are grown for food around the world isn't sustainable, or able to last. Many food-growing practices harm the planet. A third of Earth's soil has lost its **nutrients** because of overuse. If this continues, the world's topsoil, or the top layer of soil on the ground, could be gone within 60 years.

DAMAGED TOPSOIL IN DANUBE DELTA, ROMANIA

With the right tools, worldwide hunger can be wiped out.

Even now, people around the world are going hungry. Most hungry people live in low-income countries. Research shows that 55 percent of people in sub-Saharan Africa have food insecurity. About 28 percent have severe food insecurity.

A supply of safe and healthy food is a human right. **Poverty** prevents this for many, although people are working to right this wrong. With the correct knowledge and tools, we can wipe out hunger and make farming more sustainable across the world.

CHAPTER FOUR

FIXING FOOD DESERTS

A food desert is an area that doesn't have fresh food readily available. It's an urban, or city, area where there isn't fresh food within one mile (1.6 km). In a rural, or country, area, a food desert exists when there isn't fresh food within 10 miles (16.1 km).

The largest reason for food deserts is wealth inequality. Grocery store chains often move to neighborhoods with wealthier customers.

Starting in 2020, the COVID-19 pandemic affected Americans in many ways. Stores stocked less food. This and other factors increased the size and number of food deserts in the United States.

Michelle Obama (left) helps a student gather vegetables on the White House lawn.

In 2010, First Lady Michelle Obama focused on food deserts as part of the "Let's Move!" **campaign**. In 2014, Congress set aside $125 million to build supermarkets in low-income neighborhoods. While this didn't fix the problem, it was a start. To really fix food deserts, wealth must be spread more evenly around the country. This will give everyone access to healthy food.

CHAPTER FIVE

WATCHING OUR WATER FOOTPRINT

It takes a lot of Earth's natural **resources** to grow crops and raise animals. A farmer needs land and tools—and a lot of fresh water.

About 80 percent of the water used in the United States is for agriculture. However, fresh water is a limited resource. Less than 3 percent of Earth's water is fresh water. A water footprint is the amount of water an individual, company, or country uses. Two-thirds of the average American's water footprint comes from growing or raising the food we eat.

Meat has a larger water footprint than fruits, vegetables, and grains.

Raising cows uses a lot of water both for drinking and growing their food. One pound (0.4 kg) of beef takes an average of 1,800 gallons (6,813.7 L) of water to produce. In comparison, it takes about 240 gallons (908.5 L) of water to produce a loaf of bread.

CHAPTER SIX

FOOD AND FAIR TRADE

Many people love chocolate. However, the process of making chocolate can harm the environment. The chocolate industry is a major contributor to deforestation, or the removal of trees and plants to make way for building and farming.

Issues such as deforestation also cause many people to live in poverty. Unfair trade practices force farmers to sell their products at low prices and lose money.

When shopping for food, you can look for items from companies that encourage fair trade and good practices. In 2019, the World Wide Fund for Nature (WWF) worked with a food company to release a list of 50 foods that are less harmful to the environment.

CACAO BEANS

Foods from the Future 50 List

- black beans
- laver seaweed
- lentils
- buckwheat
- quinoa
- okra
- spinach
- flax seeds
- walnuts
- alfalfa sprouts

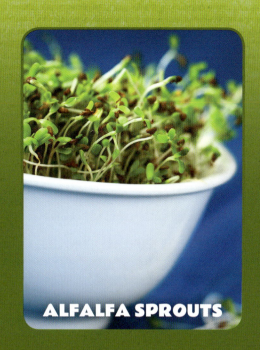

ALFALFA SPROUTS

Lentils have an environmental footprint that's 43 times smaller than that of beef.

CHAPTER SEVEN

THE AVERAGE AMERICAN DIET

In the United States, **obesity** rates and **diabetes** are among the highest in the world. More than 68 percent of all Americans are considered overweight or obese. Many Americans don't follow the food guidelines created by the U.S. Department of Agriculture (USDA) and the U.S. Department of Health and Human Services (HHS). The average American diet is high in fats and oils. Americans eat fewer fruits and vegetables than recommended.

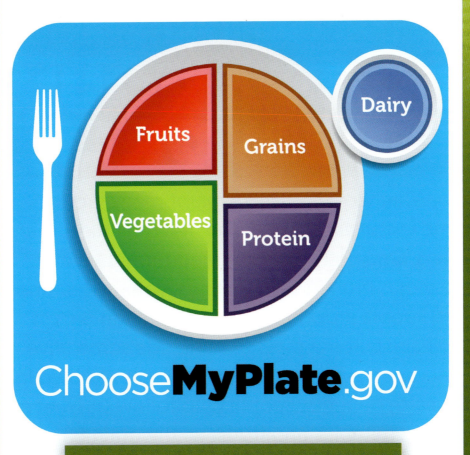

The U.S. government recommendations show that healthy meals should include fruits and vegetables.

Nutrition and overall health are very closely linked. People who don't eat well tend to have more health issues. Doctors and scientists urge people to move away from heavily processed foods, such as soda, packaged baked goods, instant soup, and instant noodles. Instead, for a healthier diet, people should eat more fresh fruits, vegetables, and nuts.

CHAPTER EIGHT

FOODS AROUND THE WORLD

What we eat is the result of many factors. Some **cultures** tend to have healthier diets than others. One of these is the Mediterranean diet. The diet is high in whole grains, vegetables, and fruit. People around the Mediterranean region also have cultural diets that include some olive oil and nuts. The Okinawan diet is also known for its health benefits. People who follow the diet eat many vegetables and fruits, whole grains, and fish. One major vegetable in the diet is sweet potatoes, which are low in calories.

MEDITERRANEAN DIET

18

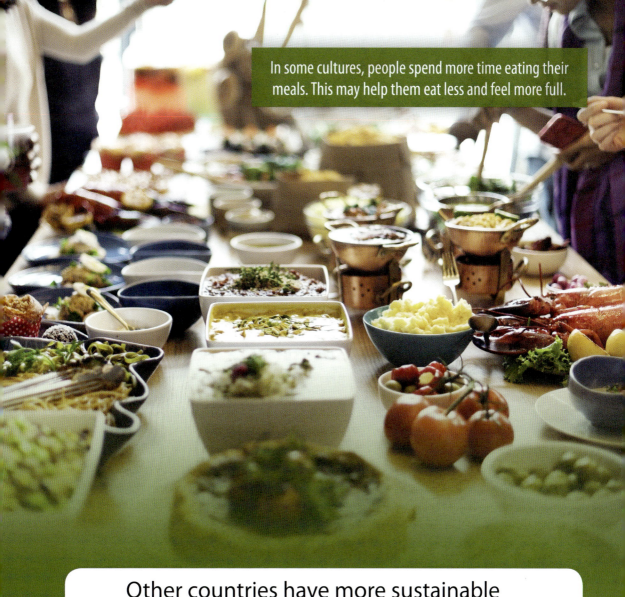
In some cultures, people spend more time eating their meals. This may help them eat less and feel more full.

   Other countries have more sustainable practices as well. Since 2016, supermarkets in France have been required to give leftover food to charities and food banks. Other countries with more sustainable food systems include the Netherlands, Canada, and Finland.

CHAPTER NINE
TO THE GROCERY STORE

On average, produce from a grocery store travels about 1,500 miles (2,414 km) to get to your plate. Food may travel by ship, plane, or truck to get to you. Often, fruits and vegetables are picked before they are ripe. This lets them travel long distances without going bad. Then, once the produce reaches stores or markets, it may be sprayed with something that makes it ripen.

When you make food purchases locally, the food is fresher. You might also be helping a local business stay open. For every $100 spent at a local business, about $68 will stay in the community. That's because local businesses are more likely to buy products and services from other local businesses. Shopping locally also keeps you more informed about how your food is grown.

Farmer's markets are a great place to buy food that was grown locally.

CHAPTER TEN

DIET AND LIFESTYLE

Making the right food choices is important. The food we eat is closely related to our health and well-being. The most important thing is to make sure you get all the nutrients you need. Still, some people eat according to fad diets, which aren't always a good thing. Balanced meals are best.

Vegetarian and vegan lifestyles are becoming more popular. Vegetarians don't generally eat meat products, but sometimes they eat eggs and dairy. Vegans generally don't eat any food or food product that came from an animal.

A good diet is an important way to keep your body healthy.

Some people choose a diet that consists of organic foods. The term "organic" refers to the way farmers grow and process food. There are strict standards that must be met for a farm to be considered organic. These include methods that don't use certain fertilizers and **pesticides**.

CHAPTER ELEVEN
THE FIGHT FOR FOOD

Young people all around the world are taking steps to help solve food problems. There's a lot one person can do. In 2014, three teenagers from Cork, Ireland, did a research project about bacteria that take nitrogen from the atmosphere and put it into the soil. This speeds up the growth of cereal crops. One of them, Sophie Healy-Thow, became further involved in agricultural practices. She's involved with an online project that helps women in agriculture in developing countries.

Maureen Muketha is also fighting to make a difference. Muketha is from Kenya. In her country, gender plays a big role in food production. In general, women do much of the planting and harvesting. Muketha has a degree in nutrition studies. She holds nutrition workshops in which she teaches women about the benefits of a varied diet.

Emer Hickey, Sophie Healy-Thow, and Ciara Judge were named the BT Young Scientists of the Year in the Royal Dublin Society.

CHAPTER TWELVE

NEW FARMING METHODS

Farmers and scientists are working on a number of new methods for producing food.

Vertical Farming

- In this method, plants are grown in different levels. This means more plants can be grown in a limited indoor space. This method uses 95 percent less water than traditional farming. However, the cost of putting this method into place concerns many people.

Plant-Based Alternatives

- Some companies have created new meat-free products that taste like meat without the high environmental impact. Some of these products have become so popular that food chains have begun serving them.

GMOs

- Scientists can alter plants by inserting different **DNA** into plant cells. People are very divided on this **technology**. Some believe genetically modified organisms, or **GMO**s, are necessary to feed a growing population. Others believe changing the DNA of food is dangerous.

The Impossible Burger is a plant-based burger that's growing in popularity. It's an environmentally friendly alternative to beef burgers.

CHAPTER THIRTEEN
HOW CAN I HELP?

There's a lot you can do to help with food issues around the world. Let leaders know how you feel about policies that are important to you. You can also change the way you live. Learn about where your food comes from and support practices you feel are best.

Ways to Get Started

- Learn about where your food comes from.
- Write letters to politicians and government officials.
- Vote with your dollar: spend where it will do the most good.
- Plant a garden in your yard or in a community space.
- Organize a food drive.
- Learn to cook meals from scratch.
- Cut down on the amount of meat you eat.
- Shop local whenever possible.
- Learn to **compost** food scraps to cut down on waste.

In 2011, Barack Obama signed a food safety policy into law. It's meant to improve the way food is handled so fewer people get sick.

CHAPTER FOURTEEN

THE FUTURE OF FOOD

The more we learn about food, the more our diets may change. Scientific discoveries will continue to change our food system in the future. As food changes happen, it's important for each of us to be aware of how our diet impacts the planet. We each need to make the right choices so that the most good can be accomplished. We must think both on a local level and on a global level.

There are many people in the United States and across the world who don't have enough to eat. We can end hunger, and we can feed ourselves in a better way. It starts with what we put on our plate. What can you do today to help create a brighter future tomorrow?

GLOSSARY

alternative (ahl-TUHR-nuh-tiv) Something that can be chosen instead of something else.

campaign (kam-PAYN) A plan to achieve a certain result.

compost (KAHM-post) To change plant material into compost, or decayed material used to improve soil.

culture (KUHL-chuhr) The beliefs and ways of life of a certain group of people.

diabetes (dy-uh-BEE-teez) A disease affecting the body's ability to produce or respond to the hormone insulin.

DNA (DEE EN AY) A matter that carries genetic information in a plant or animal's cells.

GMO (JEE EM OH) An organism that has had its DNA altered by a scientific process.

nutrient (NOO-tree-uhnt) Something taken in by a plant or animal that helps it grow and stay healthy.

obesity (oh-BEE-suh-tee) The condition of being significantly overweight.

pesticide (PEH-stuh-syd) A poison used to kill pests.

poverty (PAH-vuhr-tee) The state of being poor.

resource (REE-sohrs) A usable supply of something.

technology (tek-NAH-luh-jee) A method that uses science to solve problems and the tools used to solve those problems.

INDEX

A
Africa, 9

C
Canada, 19
Congress, U.S., 11

D
deforestation, 14
Department of Agriculture, U.S. (USDA), 16
Department of Health and Human Services (HHS), U.S., 16

F
Finland, 19
food desert, 10, 11
food insecurity, 4, 9
food scarcity, 5
France, 19

G
GMOs, 26

H
Healy-Thow, Sophie, 24
Hickey, Emer, 24

I
Ireland, 24

J
Judge, Ciera, 24
Jungle, The, 6, 7

K
Kenya, 24

M
meat, 6, 12, 29
Mediterranean diet, 18
Muketha, Maureen, 24

N
Netherlands, 19

O
Obama, Barack, 29
Obama, Michelle, 11
Okinawan diet, 18

R
Roosevelt, Theodore, 6

S
Sinclair, Upton, 7

U
United States, 10, 12, 16, 30

W
water footprint, 12

PRIMARY SOURCE LIST

Page 7
Upton Sinclair. Photograph. Ca. 1930s. Library of Congress.

Page 25
Emer Hickey, Sophie Healy-Thow, and Ciara Judge named BT Young Scientists of the Year. Photograph. Niall Carson. Dublin, Ireland. 2013. PA Images.

Page 29
President Barack Obama signs FSMA into law. Photograph. January 4, 2011. Pete Souza. Washington, D.C. 2011. White House photo.

WEBSITES

Due to the changing nature of Internet links, PowerKids Press has developed an online list of websites related to the subject of this book. This site is updated regularly. Please use this link to access the list: www.powerkidslinks.com/SOOF/feeding